This book belongs to

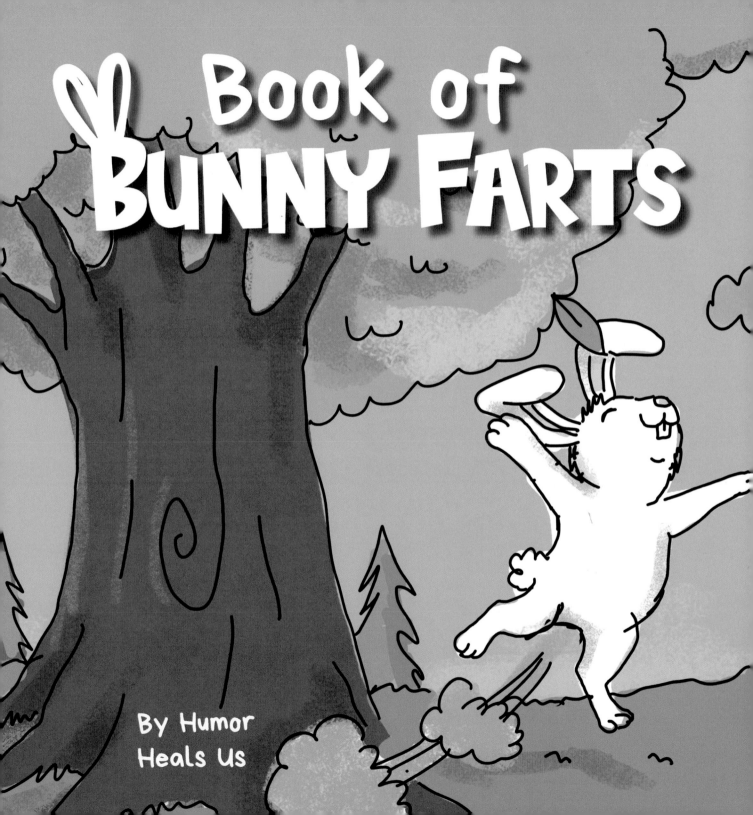

Book of
BUNNY FARTS

By Humor
Heals Us

Hi, I'm the Easter Bunny.
I deliver up to 3 billion eggs a year.
How do I get all that energy, you ask?

I eat... a lot!

All that eating gives me plenty of gas. Yes, it smells, but I couldn't survive without gas. So you could say it's essential. My gas comes in many different forms. Let me explain...

Jelly Beans

Beans, beans are good for your heart.
The more you eat, the more you fart!

Sometimes, I can hear noises in my stomach. When the gas chooses to go up through my mouth instead of the other way, it's an **egg-cellent surprise**!

Hop-pity-hop

These farts give me energy to keep hopping all day long!

If a kid has found some eggs in the flower garden, I can also just blame it on some **funny smelling flowers**.

Lost Ducklings

The truth is sometimes the gas makes others confused and I admit that's not very nice.

Mellow Marshmallow

These farts are soft and silent. It's a good thing because they really, really stink!

The truth is my gas does smell, but I can blame it on the **putrid pastel** rotten eggs!

Putrid Pastels

Have you ever had this feeling? You know something big is about to come out of your butt and so you run for some privacy but it escapes anyway? Then, you've experienced a **bunny train**!

There's one more fart I like to do. It's called an egg explosion. It comes out so forcefully that I'm so grateful there are fireworks nearby to mask the sounds.

As you can see, being the Easter Bunny is a BIG responsibility.

Now, if you'll excuse me, I have some business to attend to.

Don't forget farting is healthy for you.

If you don't believe me, just refer to our next book – Foxy the Fox's Fourth of July Firework Farts.

To be continued...

Follow us on FB and IG @humorhealsus
To vote on new title names and freebies, visit
us at humorhealsus.com for more information.

@humorhealsus   @humorhealsus